3-D THRILLERS!

HUMAN BODY

PAUL HARRISON

ARCTURUS

What a Wonderful

You probably take it for granted, but your body is a truly wonderful thing. Look at all the things that make you what you are: skin, hair, blood, muscles, organs, veins – to name just some of the bits. And what's more it all fits together in one neat package. Take a closer look at your body and you'll be really surprised what's going on in there.

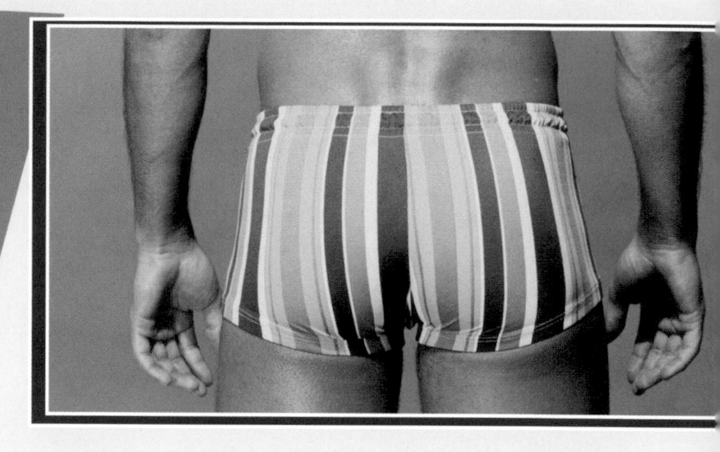

▲ BIG AND SMALL

Your body is a combination of large and small pieces. The largest muscle in your body is your gluteus maximus, but you might find it a bit difficult to see exactly how big it is because it's behind you – it's your bottom. The smallest bone in your body is the stirrup bone, which is only 2 millimetres long and is inside your ear.

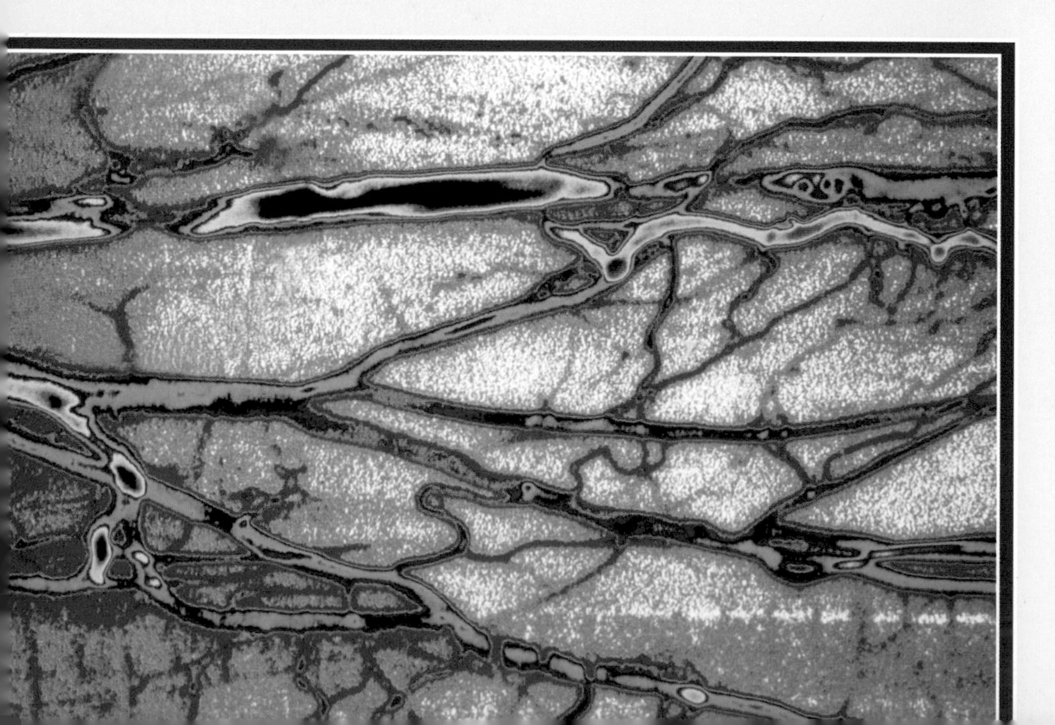

◄ TUBES

Your body is stuffed full of tubes, or veins as they are called, and this is how the blood travels around your body. If you could take all the veins out of a body and lay them end to end they would stretch for around 100,000 kilometres! That's long enough to wrap around the Moon nine times!

Body

► STRETCHY

Apart from having all those miles of veins and hundreds of different bits and pieces, your body is also fantastically flexible. From birth, you will grow for around 18 years and be about five times longer than you were when you were born. Even when you're fully grown you can still expand. Think about a pregnant woman and how her womb has to get bigger to accommodate that baby – her body needs to be really stretchy to allow the bump to stick out.

A cell is like a microscopic chemical package. Your body is made up of millions of cells – so many that scientists can't really say how many there are.

◄ OVERCOMING THE FLAWS

Although the way the body works is just one of nature's marvels, it's not perfect. For a start, we have quite large heads, which we need to fit our oh-so-intelligent brains into. Unfortunately all this weight at the top of our relatively long bodies makes us quite unstable – that's why toddlers fall down so often. However, as we've survived this long, there can't be too much wrong with us!

Super Structure

That wonderful body of yours would be nothing but a sack of blood and organs without your bones. It's our arrangement of bones that makes humans look like humans, but that's not the only job bones do – your skeleton is really a super structure.

► MISSING BONES?

You have a lot more bones than you probably realize; in fact you have a whopping 206 of them. But before you get too pleased with yourself, that's nothing compared to babies – they've got over 300 bones. So where do these extra bones go? Nowhere, is the answer; babies' bones are quite soft and many of them fuse together before they harden, reducing the number to just over 200 as they grow older.

◄ HARD SPONGE

Your bones may hold you up, but they are not solid – if they were they'd be very heavy. The inside of our bones looks a bit like a honeycomb or a sponge – it's filled with loads of tiny holes. This has the advantage of making your bones both strong and light. This honeycomb structure is surrounded by a smooth, hard outside which is the bit you can see when you look at the bone.

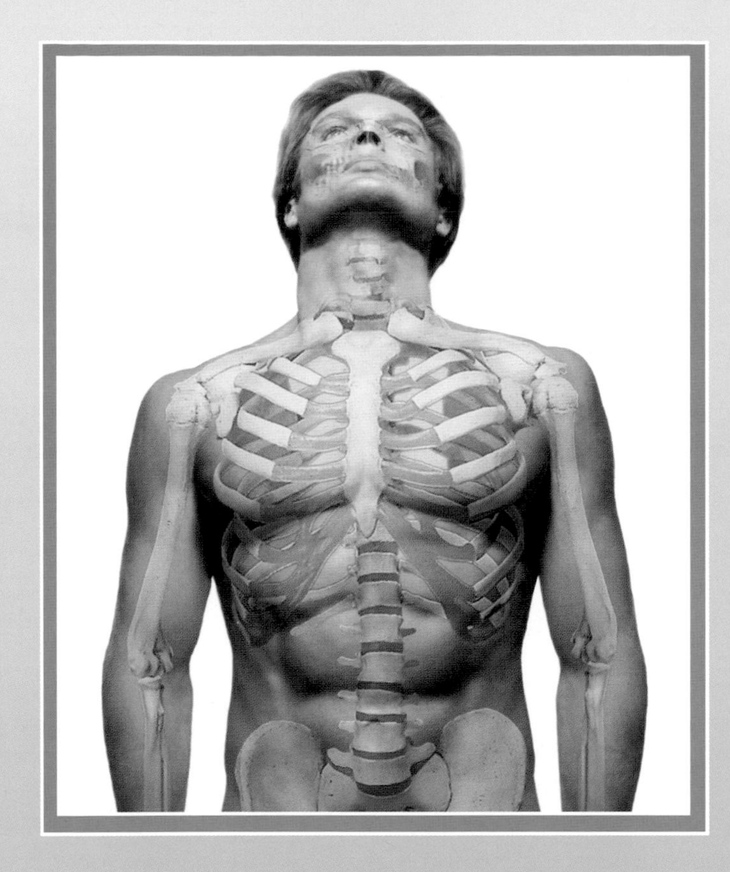

◄ MULTI-TASKING

Your bones don't just make you human-shaped; they perform other important roles, too. The way your bones are arranged to make your skeleton means they provide a useful protection service. For instance, your ribs protect your lungs and heart and your skull protects your brain. That's not all; inside your bones is a substance called marrow and this produces your blood cells – you'll find out more about what they do later on.

Some young bones are made from cartilage, which is the same stuff that a shark's skeleton is made from (and the bit at the end of your nose).

◄ GROWING

Obviously, as you grow up your bones get bigger – otherwise you'd stay child-sized forever. In fact, your bones continue to get bigger until your late teens. But when you reach your 20s it doesn't mean that that's it. Your bones are always renewing themselves; old bits of bone dissolve and new bits replace them. It's just as well the new bits grow – you know what we'd look like without any bones!

On the Inside

Everything inside your body is there for a reason, but some of the most important components are your organs. These are individual bits of the body that do a specific job. You've got quite a few of them in your body, but here are some of the major ones.

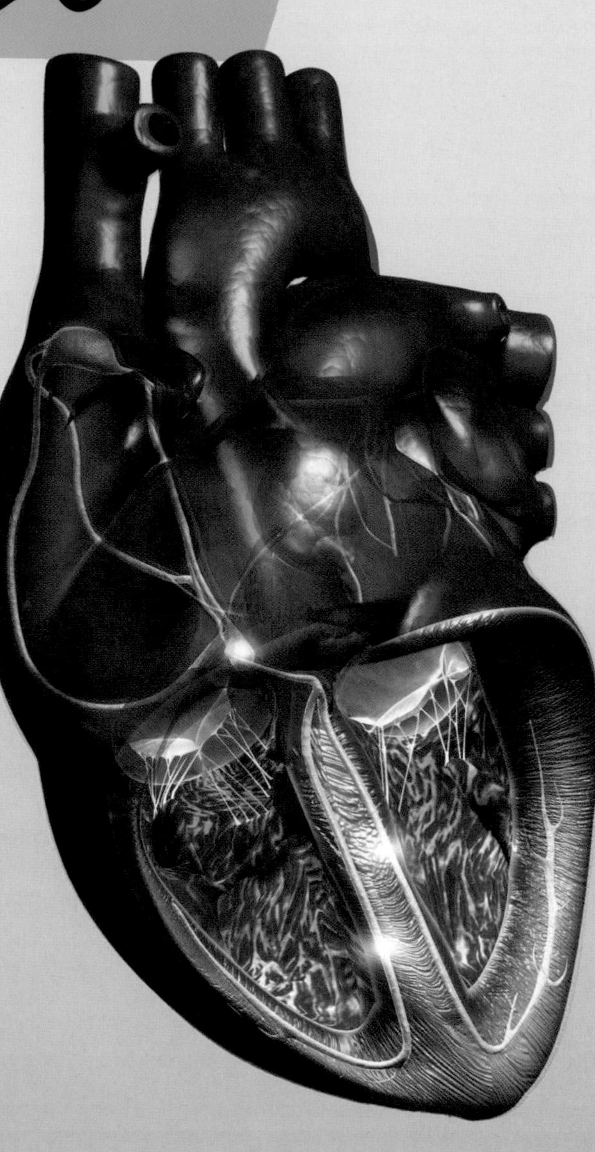

HEART OF THE MATTER ►

The heart is a muscle which moves the blood around your body. The blood flows into the heart through the veins, passing through four different chambers inside it before exiting the heart through other veins. When you feel your heart beating it is the muscle pumping the blood from one chamber to the next. It does this around 70 times a minute and never stops, day or night – if it does you're in big trouble!

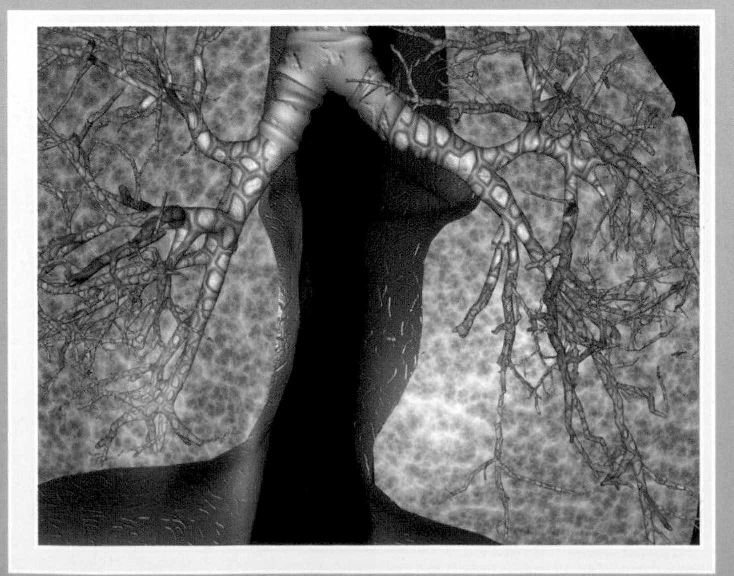

◄ DEEP BREATH

Every time you take a breath you can feel your lungs at work as they make your chest move as they fill with air. Your lungs aren't like big air-filled balloons though – it's more a case of a big bag with lots of little bags inside it. The lungs are filled with little veins and tiny air sacs, which in turn are surrounded by blood vessels. The vessels take the air from the sacs and move it around your body.

KIDNEYS ►

Your kidneys are two fist-sized organs that are the waste-reprocessing plant of your body. They take all the bits your body doesn't need from your blood and gets rid of any extra water. The kidneys send this liquid waste to the bladder were it's stored until you go to the toilet. The kidneys also control the amount of various chemicals in your blood – too many would be bad news, so these little organs have a big job to do.

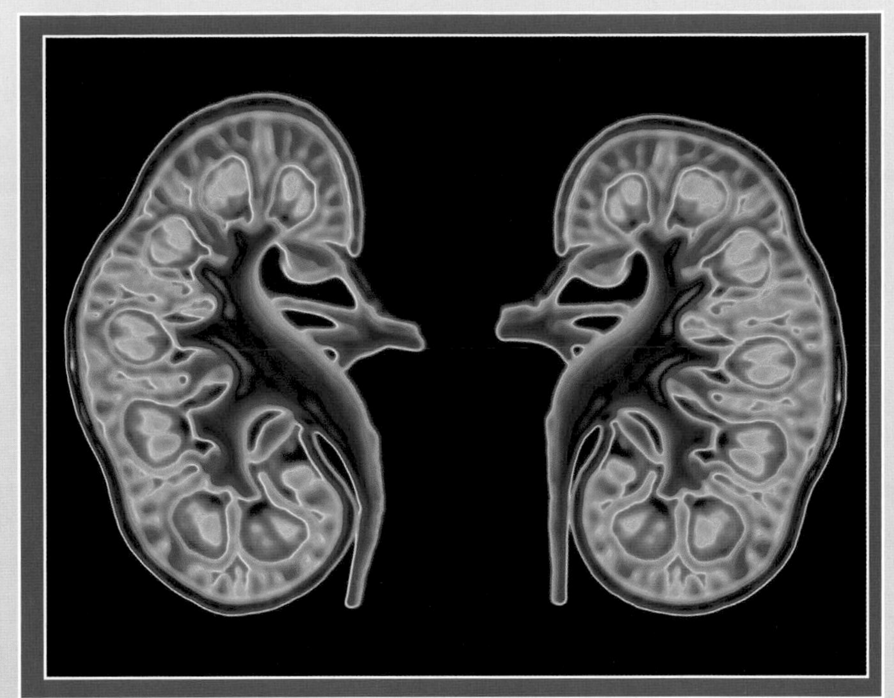

One organ you have but don't need anymore is your appendix. Some scientists think it helped our ancestors to digest tough food that humans no longer eat.

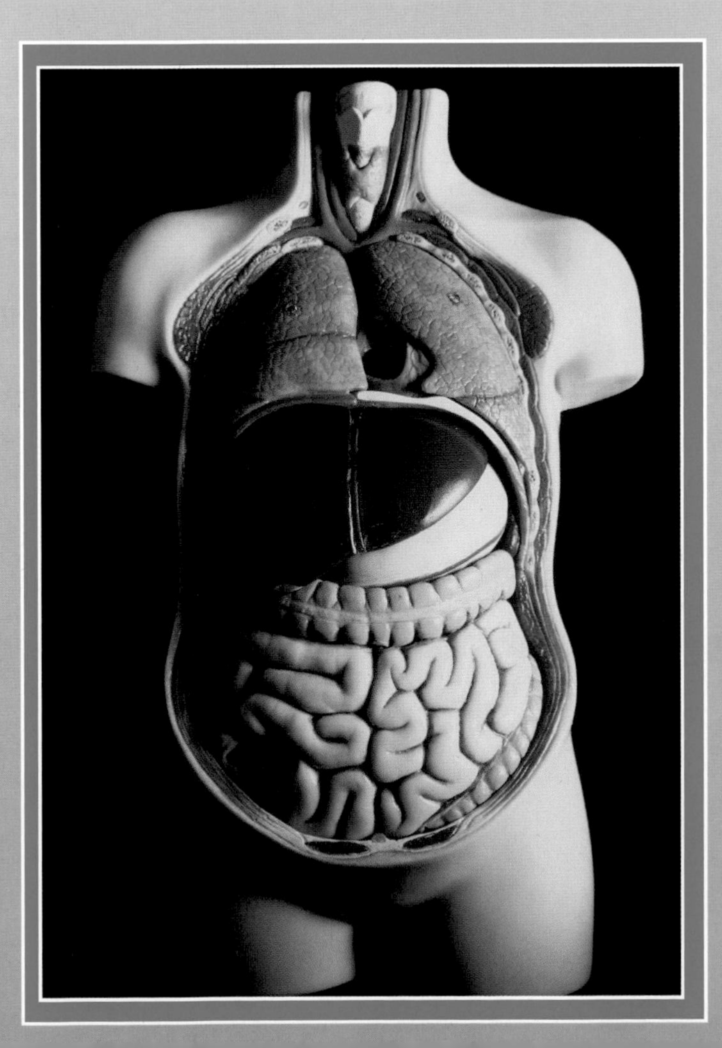

◄ HARD-WORKING LIVER

The biggest organ inside your body is your liver. It works a bit like a big factory making chemicals that your body needs from the nutrients that you eat. It also helps to guard the body by producing the substance that allows the blood to clot – which is handy, as without this we'd bleed to death if we got cut. The liver also produces bile, which helps the body to digest the food you eat. With so many jobs, it's not surprising the liver is so big.

On the Outside

All those bones, blood vessels, tubes and organs would be just one big mess on the floor if it wasn't for your skin to keep it all in. But don't think for one minute your skin is just a big bag – it's much more interesting than that.

STRETCHY ORGAN ►

Your skin is actually your body's biggest organ and does some really important jobs. It acts like a living suit of armour, keeping out germs and harmful ultraviolet rays from the sun. It also acts as a layer of insulation, keeping the body at a reasonable temperature as well as keeping water out.

◄ STRAIGHT OR CURLY?

The holes in our skin that hair comes out of are called follicles. You've got loads of them – over a million in fact – and the shape of your follicles decides what kind of hair you have. A curly shaped follicle results in curly hair and a straight follicle means straight hair.

BUMPS ►

The hair which grows out of your skin adds another level of insulation, but we have a lot less hair than our ancient ancestors used to – manly because we don't need it anymore. It's also the reason we get goosebumps. When our bodies get cold the skin contracts and this pushes the hair up off the skin. In furry animals this would increase the amount of air trapped between the hairs which would help to keep them warm. On our not-so-hairy bodies all it does is give us bumpy skin.

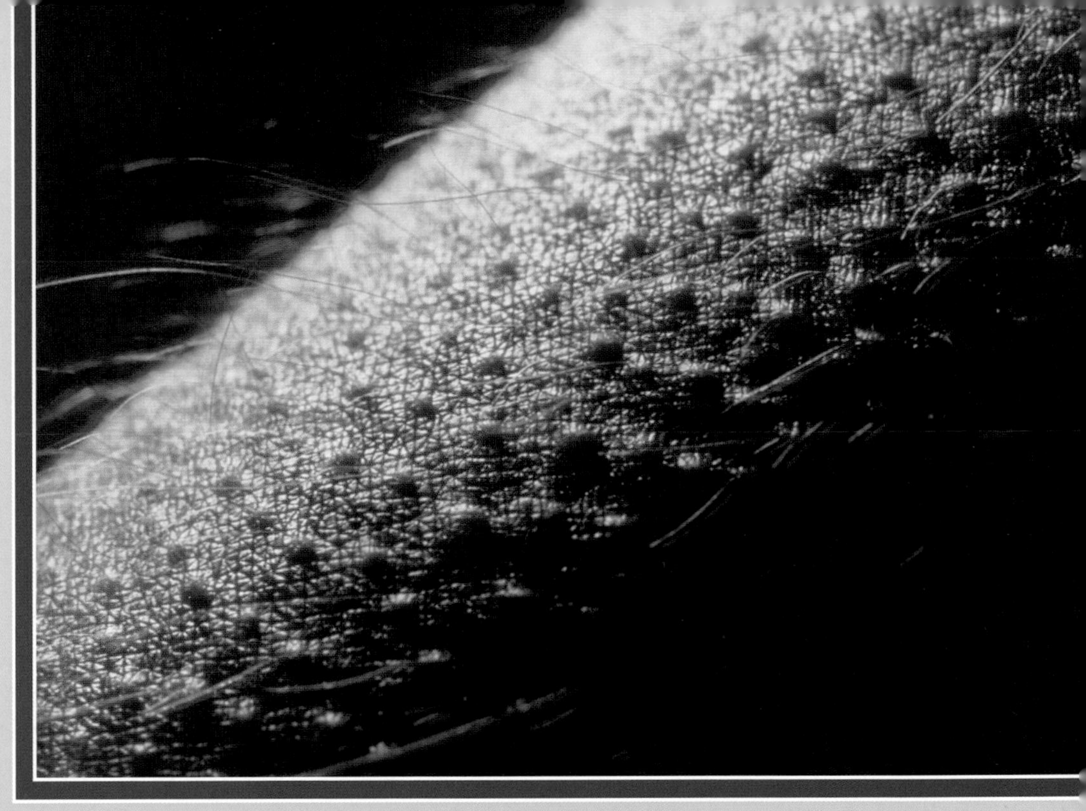

Your skin is dying and re-growing all of the time – a lot of the dust you see around you is actually dead skin!

LAYER UPON LAYER ►

Your skin is actually made of three separate layers and they all do different things. The outside layer is called the epidermis and keeps everything outside the body from getting inside. The middle layer, or the dermis as it is called, is where your hair grows from. It also has all your sweat glands – sweating is your body's way of cooling down. The bottom layer, or hypodermis, is there to keep your skin attached to the rest of your body. Without the hypodermis your skin would hang off your bones like an old sack – not a good look.

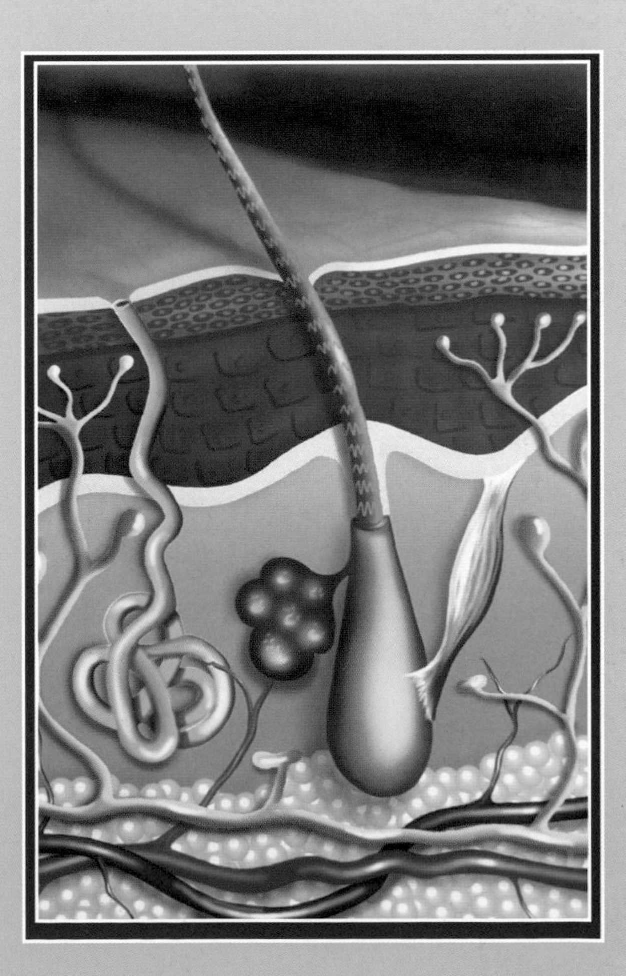

Sense and Sensibility

Your senses provide you with awareness of the world around you. Without them you wouldn't know what was around you – which would be a problem if you were being stalked by a tiger, for example. So your senses really do make sense.

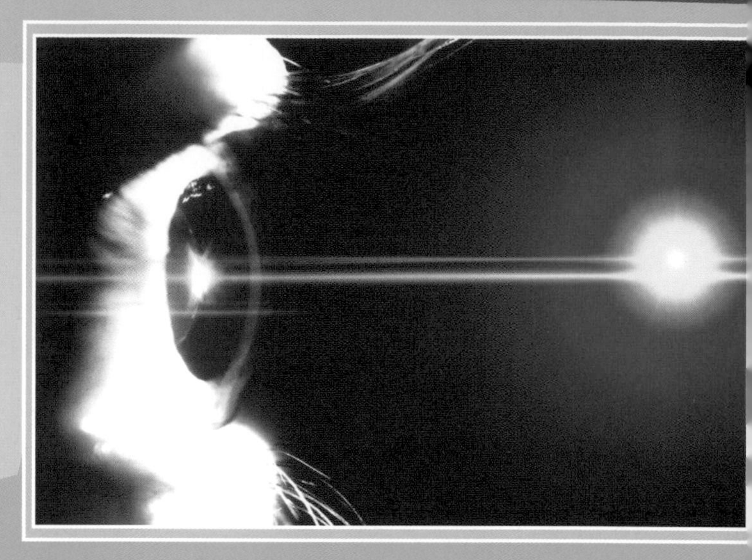

▲ EYE EYE

There's a lot going on when you look at something. The light coming from the image of what you are looking at enters the eye, where it's flipped upside down and is projected onto the back of your eye onto something called the retina. This signal travels to your brain along the optic nerve where the brain flips the image the right way up. Your eyes also tell you how far away an object is and what colour it is. Staring at one thing for too long can strain the eyes, which is all the reason you need not to watch too much telly – those eyes need protecting!

▼ TOUCHY FEELY

Your body is covered in thousands of nerve endings found in the bottom layer of your skin. These send messages to the brain whenever your skin touches something. Most of your touch receptors are grouped in specific parts of your body such as your fingertips and your tongue. This is handy – imagine if you had to rub your bottom on everything to find out what it felt like!

STINKY ►

Your ability to taste things wouldn't be anywhere near as good if you couldn't smell them. Your nose is much more discerning than your tongue and can pick out hundreds of different smells. In fact, your sense of taste and smell are so closely linked that food doesn't taste the same if you've got a blocked nose. Smells are also very good at triggering memories, but we're not entirely sure why this useful.

Generally people think that there are only five senses - but there are more. Most scientists would add the ability to feel heat, cold, pain, and balance to the list.

◄ TASTY!

Your ability to taste things rests – literally – on your tongue, which is covered in tiny taste receptors. When you think of all the different flavours of things you like to eat you'd think that these receptors must be pretty complex, but in fact they can only distinguish between five different tastes – bitter, sweet, sour, salt and umami. This last one sounds a bit odd, but it is a specific taste that comes with many foods including meat and cheese. So if you like cheeseburgers, these taste receptors will be working pretty hard.

Brain Box

You can remove pretty much everything from your body – including your heart – and replace it for a while with a machine and keep on living. But take out your brain and there's nothing that can replace it. That's because your brain keeps the whole show on the road.

TAXI!

Different thoughts or actions are dealt with by different parts of your brain. The right-hand side is responsible for your creative side, while the left-hand side is in charge of the more logical and scientific stuff. What's more, if you use one area of your brain a lot it gets bigger. Famously, London taxi drivers have to remember lots of streets and routes and as a result the bit of their brain they use to remember such things is bigger than average.

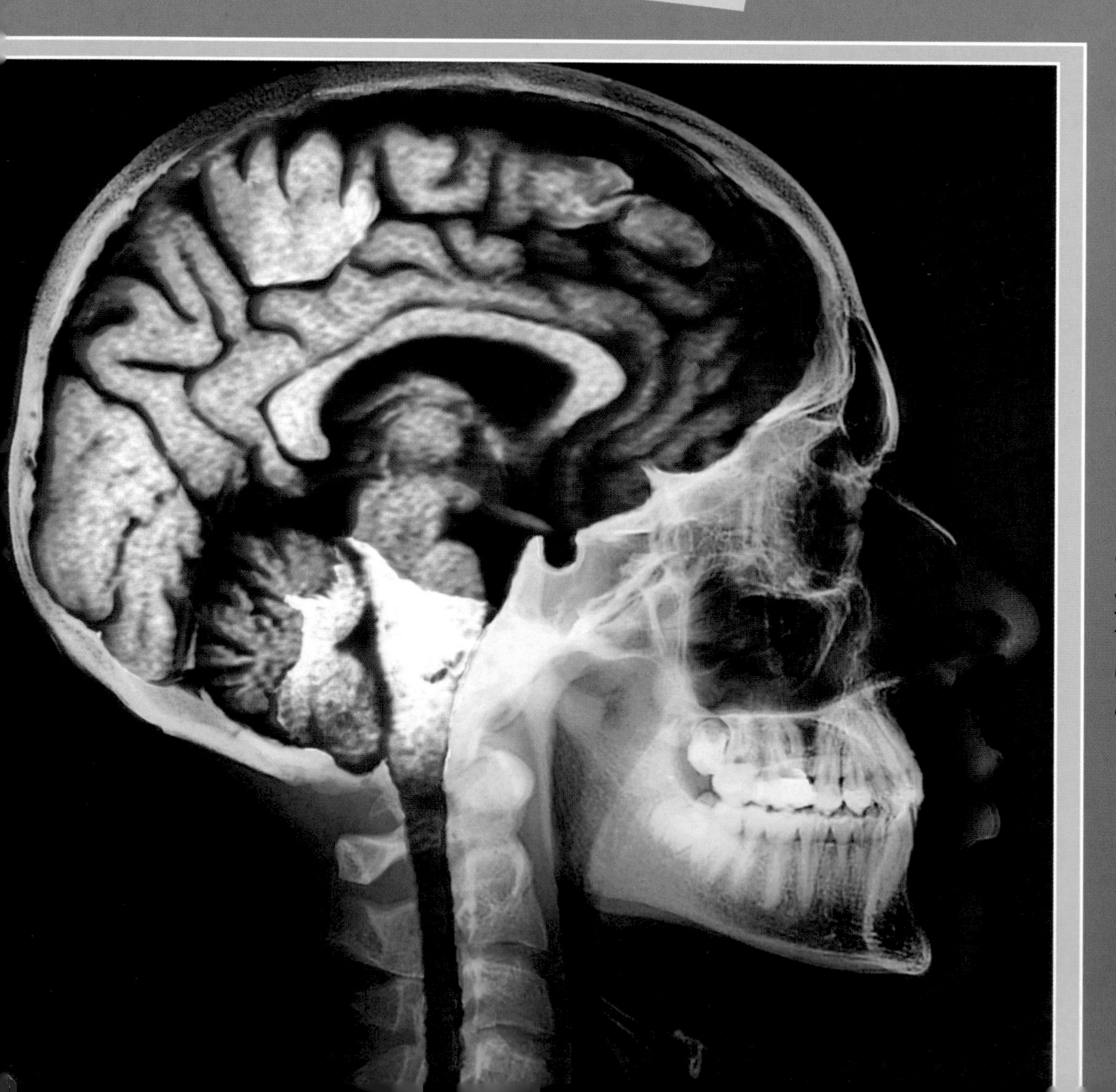

◄ WHAT IT DOES

Your brain is really your body's very own super computer. It processes all the information that your senses send it, from what you're touching to the upside-down images on your retina. Your brain does all your thinking, and governs your movements, controls your breathing and stores your memories. Like your heart, it works 24/7 – when you're asleep your brain doesn't knock off for the night too. In fact, when you dream, your brain is just as active as it is during the day.

GLOWING ►

Scientists don't know exactly how the brain works, but they can monitor brain activity using special scanners. The scanners show scientists and doctors which bits of the brain are active by lighting up the areas being used. This helps our understanding of how the brain works – as well as providing some very pretty pictures of the brain.

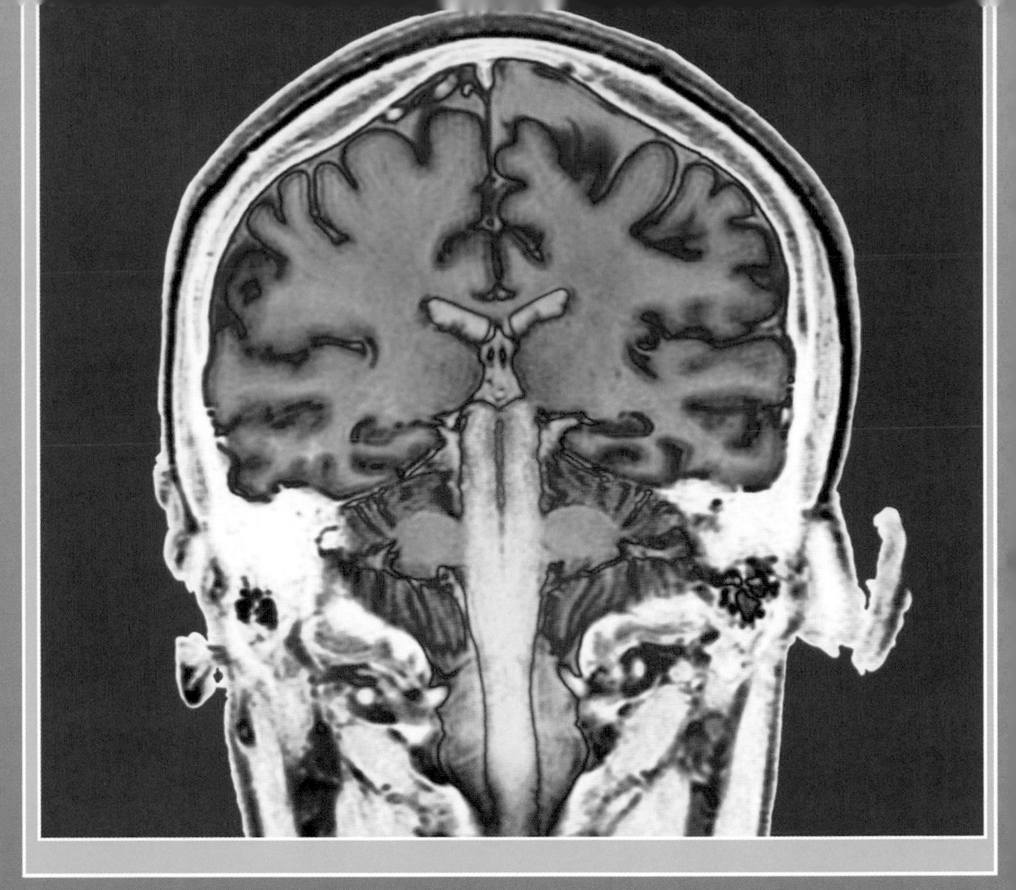

The more you use your brain the better it works – but don't think too much, as it really can tire your brain out!

◄ WHAT IT LOOKS LIKE

For such a vital bit of your body, your brain doesn't look like much – it looks a bit like a squidgy peach stone. There are three separate parts to your brain. The cerebrum is the largest part and this bit is split into two halves called hemispheres. Below that is a part called the cerebellum, and coming out from the bottom is the brain stem. As the brain is so important, it is protected by the skull, and to stop the brain bashing against the skull it is surrounded by thin membranes and fluid. Even then, a bad bash on the head can damage your brain – you wouldn't drop a computer on the floor, so you have to be careful with your brain, too.

Under Attack

Like any other fantastic machine, your body has to be well looked after. What makes things difficult is that your body is under constant attack – and a lot of the time you can't even see what's attacking you.

WIGGLY WORMS ►

The world is crammed full of bacteria, but you wouldn't know as it is microscopically small. Bacteria are everywhere, even inside our bodies. Some of it is good and helps us, but some of it can make us ill if it gets inside us. That's not the only threat; you can accidentally swallow very tiny eggs which can grow into things like worms which – and this is really disgusting – like nowhere better to live than inside your stomach and intestines. Some of them even pop their heads out of your bottom at night to lay their eggs!

◄ KEEP OUT!

Your body has a number of ways of tackling disease and suchlike. Obviously the best thing to do is to stop them from getting into your body in the first place. That first layer of defence is one of the main jobs your skin does, but that's not your only natural barrier. Inside your nose and throat you have special tissues that produce mucus – or what you might call snot. The mucus traps bacteria that you breathe in. So next time you complain about a blocked nose just remember that most of the time that snot is doing you good.

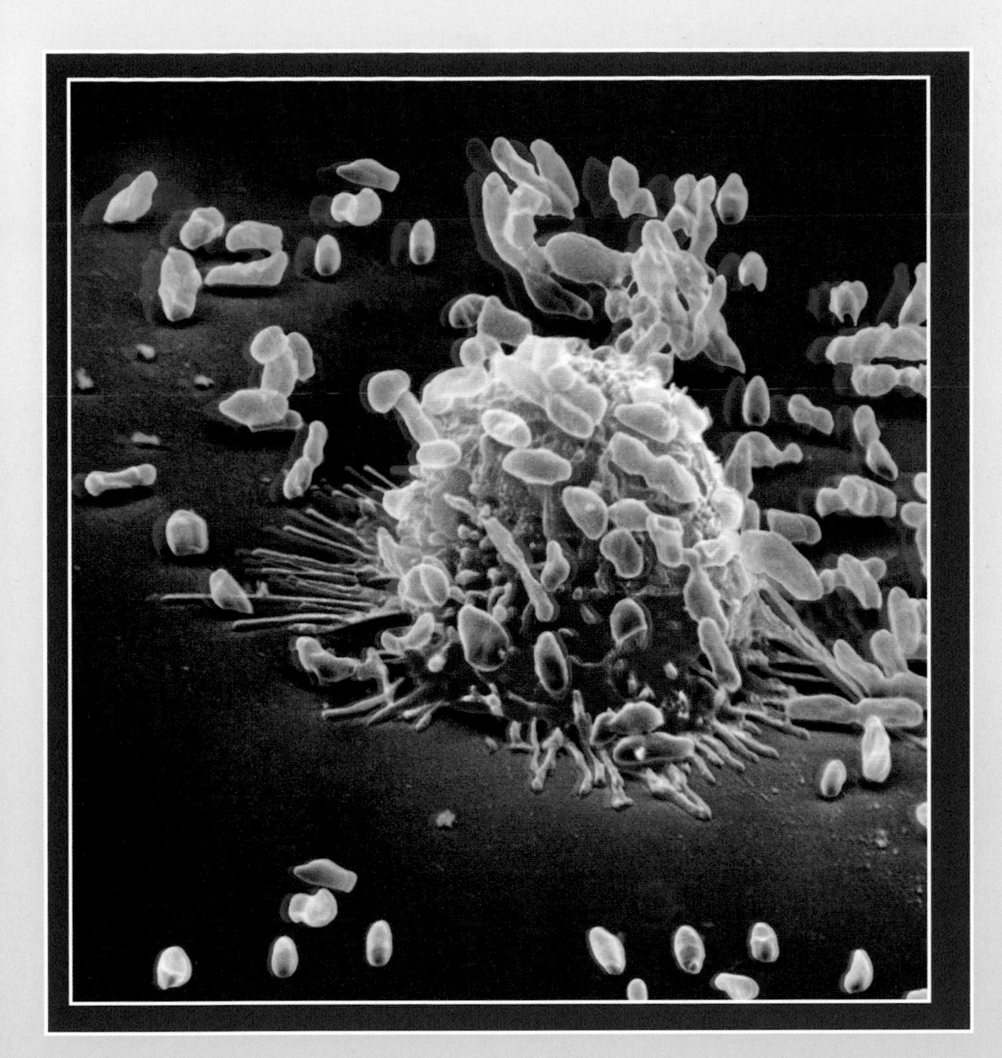

◄ WHITE BLOOD CELLS

Despite all the barriers, harmful bacteria will always get into your body; but then your blood comes into play. Your blood is made up of red and white blood cells. The red cells move the oxygen around your body while the white cells act like security guards. They are on the lookout for harmful bacteria and get rid of them by swallowing them up.

One of the simplest and most effective ways of reducing the risk of bacteria getting into your body is to wash your hands regularly.

LOOKING AFTER NUMBER ONE ►

Although your body is really good at looking after itself, it still needs a helping hand. Basically, the better you look after yourself, the better you'll feel. And it's not difficult. Eating fresh fruit and vegetables gives your body the vitamins it needs to help fight bacteria. Regular exercise gets the lungs and heart working better and pumps the blood through your veins. And getting plenty of sleep helps the brain to organize all your thoughts. A better rested and fitter body is in a better position to tackle diseases, so for the sake of your own wellbeing, hop to it!

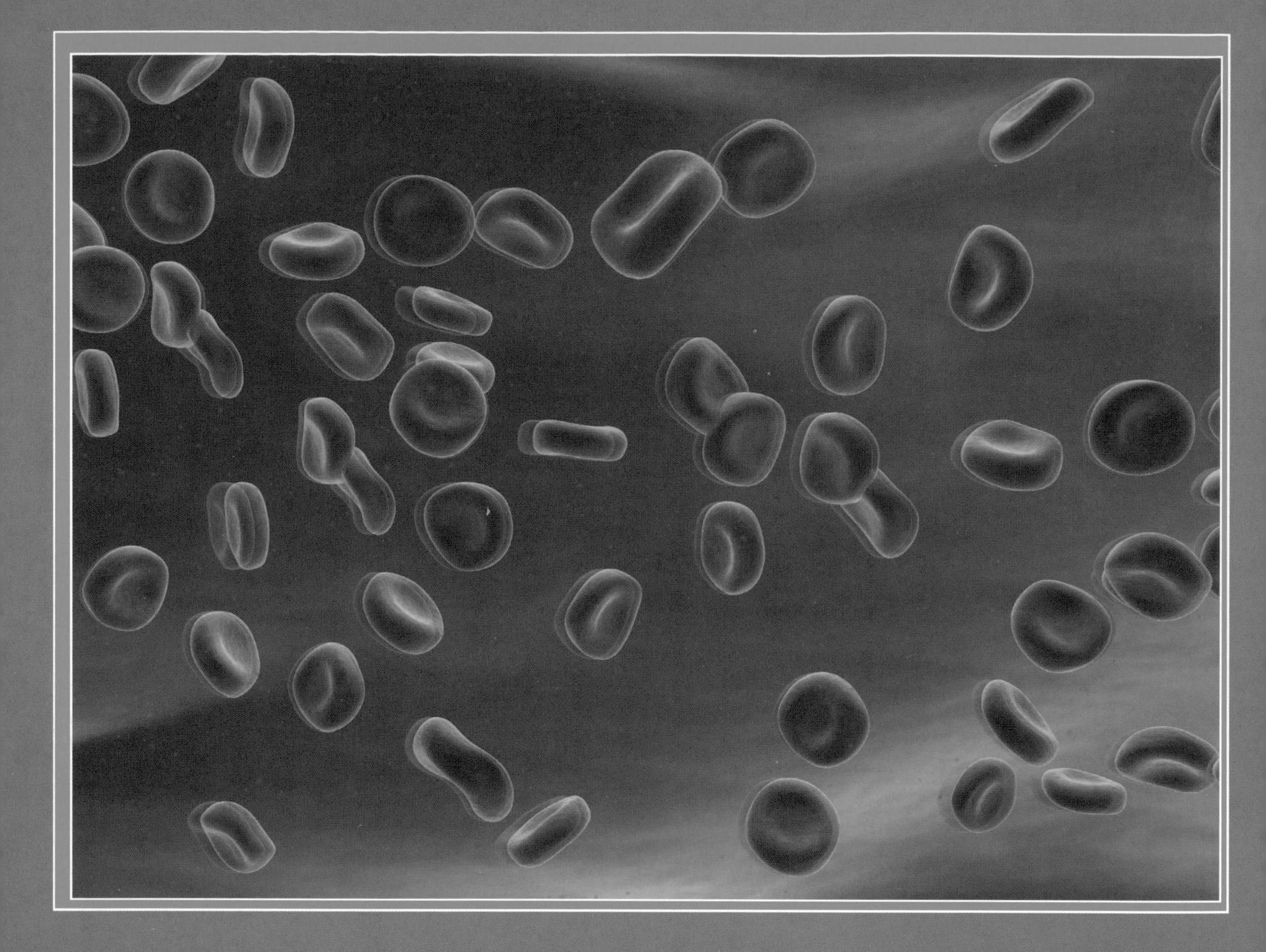

This edition published in 2010 by Arcturus Publishing Limited
26/27 Bickels Yard, 151–153 Bermondsey Street,
London SE1 3HA

Author: Paul Harrison
Editor: Fiona Tulloch

Picture credits:
Corbis: page 2, top and bottom; page 11, bottom; page 14, bottom left.
Getty Images: page 4, left; page 6, top and bottom; page 15, bottom right.
Nature Picture Library: page 10, bottom left.
Rex Features: page 3, bottom; page 8, bottom.
Science Photo Library: page 4, right; page 5, top left; page 7, top and bottom; page 9, top and bottom; page 10, top right; page 12; page 13, top and bottom; page 14, top right; page 15, top left.

3D images by Pinsharp 3D Graphics

Printed in China

ISBN: 978-1-84193-734-2
CH000518EN

Supplier 03, Date 0910, Print Run 450